Ice Cream

BEFORE THE STORE

BY JAN BERNARD • ILLUSTRATED BY DAN McGEEHAN

Published by The Child's World®
1980 Lookout Drive • Mankato, MN 56003-1705
800-599-READ • www.childsworld.com

ACKNOWLEDGMENTS
The Child's World®: Mary Berendes, Publishing Director
The Design Lab: Design and production
Red Line Editorial: Editorial direction
Content Consultant: Kyle W. Stiegert, Professor and Director of Food System Research Group,
    University of Wisconsin-Madison

ISBN 9781609736774
LCCN 2011940073

PHOTO CREDITS
Olga Lyubkin/Dreamstime, cover, 1, back cover; Caroline Henri/Dreamstime, cover (inset), 1 (inset);
Dusan Zidar/Shutterstock Images, 5; Pangfolio.com/Shutterstock Images, 7, 30; BanksPhotos/
iStockphoto, 9; Sean Shot/iStockphoto, 11; Jonathan Sloane/iStockphoto, 13; Alain Couillaud/
iStockphoto, 17; iStockphoto, 21, 31 (top); Mykhaylo Feshchur/Shutterstock Images, 23; Stephen
Coburn/Bigstock, 29, 31 (bottom)

Design elements: Olga Lyubkin/Dreamstime

Printed in the United States of America

ABOUT THE AUTHOR

Jan Bernard has been an elementary teacher in both Ohio and Georgia and has written curriculum for schools for more than seven years. She lives in West Jefferson, Ohio, with her husband, Tom, and their dog, Nigel. She has two sons who live in Columbus, Ohio.

Contents

CHAPTER ONE

Sweet Ice Cream

Yum! A sweet chocolate ice cream cone is the perfect treat on a hot day. How about a thick strawberry milkshake? Ice cream comes in so many flavors. Some kinds have swirls and some have chunks. Do you like to pour caramel sauce on top? Or do you prefer sprinkles and nuts? Ice cream is delicious however you like it!

Ice cream comes in many delicious flavors.

Have you thought about how ice cream is made? There are many steps in the process. The first step starts at a dairy farm. That is where cows spend their days eating grass, alfalfa, and corn. They use part of the energy they get from this food to make milk. That is important, because milk is the main **ingredient** in ice cream!

Ice cream begins with cows on a dairy farm.

CHAPTER TWO

At the Dairy Farm

Dairy cows are milked every day. Farmers lead the cows into milking stalls. A milking machine is hooked up to their udders to take the milk. A single cow can give about 55 to 60 pounds (25 to 27 kg) of milk a day. Farmers are paid by the pound for milk and not by the gallon.

A gallon of milk weighs about 8.5 pounds (4 kg).

Machines are used to milk cows.

Milk is warm when it comes out of a cow. The milk is quickly put into milk holding tanks. This keeps it from spoiling. These tanks are like your refrigerator at home, only much bigger. Every few days, a refrigerated **tanker truck** visits the dairy farm. The milk in the holding tanks is piped into the tanker truck. The truck then takes the milk to its next stop—the ice cream factory.

Refrigerated tanker trucks take milk from the dairy.

CHAPTER THREE

An Ice Cream Factory

Once the milk arrives at the factory, it is tested. The tests show if the milk is fresh and safe. Workers also see how much butterfat is in the milk. Butterfat is another name for cream. Milk comes from different dairies. The milk is mixed together and stored in large cold storage bins. Next, the milk is separated into cream and **skimmed** milk.

Milk and cream are stored in storage tanks.

Now it's time to make the basic ice cream mix. A worker uses a very large blender to mix together the main ingredients. What are those ingredients? They are cream, skimmed milk, sweeteners, and **stabilizers**.

Cream is a very important part of the ice cream mix. More cream makes ice cream taste good. It also makes ice cream smoother and thicker. Adding more cream also makes the ice cream cost more.

Skimmed milk makes ice cream good for you. It has protein, calcium, vitamins, and minerals that your body needs.

Sweeteners give ice cream a sweet taste. Cane sugar or beet sugar are often used. So are corn sweeteners and even honey.

Ice cream mix is made with different ingredients.

Stabilizers come from different parts of plants. They are used in very small amounts. They keep **ice crystals** from forming in the ice cream. When ice crystals form in ice cream it can feel sandy or gritty in your mouth. You don't want that!

These main ingredients make the ice cream mix. It only needs to blend for a few minutes. Once that is done, it's time for the next step.

Next two important things happen to the mix. It is **pasteurized** and **homogenized**. When the mix is pasteurized, it is heated. This kills **bacteria** in the mix.

Raw milk is milk as it comes right out of the cow. It can make people sick, because it contains bacteria.

A large machine is used in pasteurization.

Bacteria are very tiny living things. They are all around us all the time. We need some kinds of bacteria to keep us healthy. Good bacteria help us digest our food better. But some bacteria can make us very sick. That is the kind of bacteria that is sometimes found in raw milk. The mix is heated to 161 F (72 C) for 15 seconds. That's all it takes. And the bacteria in the ice cream will be gone.

Homogenization is the next step. Cream often separates from other ingredients. To stop this, the cream is broken into very tiny bits. This makes the

cream stay mixed with the other ingredients. That's exactly what ice cream makers want! A large machine called a homogenizer is used. The ice cream mix is shot into the homogenizer with high pressure. The pressure breaks up the cream. After the mix is homogenized, it is cooled quickly. Then it sits for four hours or more.

A homogenization machine is used to break up the cream.

CHAPTER FOUR

Yummy Flavors

Why do we eat ice cream? Because it tastes so good! That means the next step is really important. At this point the mix does not have much flavor. It is mostly just sweet milk and cream. When the mix goes into large flavor vats, different flavors are added. Some ice cream will become vanilla. Some ice cream will become chocolate. Some other flavors that can be added include peach, peppermint, and strawberry. Coloring can also be added to the vats.

Ice cream flavors are mixed in large batches.

The mixture is then pumped into a large mixing freezer. Inside the freezer, blades turn while air is added to the mix. Adding air is important. Without some air mixed in, your ice cream would be about as hard as an ice cube!

If the ice cream is not going to have anything else added, it is ready to go into cartons. But if it is going to be a chunky ice cream, it goes through a feeder. The feeder is a machine that puts chunks into ice cream. Everything from crumbled cookies to strawberry pieces to peanuts can be added. The ice

cream might have swirls. Chocolate fudge or peanut butter are two kinds of swirls. If swirls are added, the ice cream goes through another machine. It melts the swirl mixture to a certain temperature. Then it is smoothly mixed into the ice cream.

Flavors, swirls, and chunks are added to the ice cream mixture.

CHAPTER FIVE

Into the Cartons

Now it is time to fill the cartons! Machines called fillers quickly fill cartons with ice cream as they move along a **conveyor belt**. Next a machine puts a lid on each of the cartons. Finally the cartons pass under an ink jet. It prints the date the ice cream **expires** onto each carton.

But the ice cream is not ready to leave the factory. It next has to be hardened. That means it has to be frozen solid. Then the ice cream is less

The cartons are filled with ice cream.

likely to melt during shipment. The cartons are put into a spiral hardener. A spiral hardener is a freezing machine that can be a tall as a two-story building. It has a conveyor belt that spirals upward through the machine. As the cartons go up, fans blast cold air. When the cartons come out, they are frozen solid.

Ice cream cartons next need to be packaged. They are bundled together by flavor and wrapped in plastic for shipping. The ice cream packages are called sleeves. The sleeves are then packed on large pallets.

Ice cream batches must be tasted before leaving the factory. Random cartons are also tested to make sure the ice cream is safe to eat.

A spiral hardener freezes the ice cream solid.

CHAPTER SIX

Into Your Bowl

When a batch of ice cream passes its tests, the ice cream cartons can be shipped. The pallets are loaded onto refrigerated trucks. Then they are shipped to your grocery store. If you are on the hunt for your favorite ice cream flavor, go to the freezer section. Check out all the choices you have! Will you choose rocky road or butter pecan? Or how about vanilla fudge ripple? You can choose one that is extra creamy. Or you can try one that is low in fat. There are a lot of delicious choices to make when picking ice cream.

Pick your favorite. Then stick it in your freezer at home. For your next treat, grab a big bowl, scoop in some ice cream, and add some toppings. That's all you need to make a big ice cream sundae. Grab a spoon and dig in!

Ice cream is kept in the freezer section of the grocery store.

ICE CREAM MAP

1 DAIRY FARM

2 MAKE ICE CREAM MIX

3

MIX IN FLAVORS

4

PUT INTO CARTONS

5

SHIP TO GROCERY STORES

GLOSSARY

bacteria (bak-TIHR-ee-uh): Bacteria are small living things that are harmful or helpful. Pasteurization kills harmful bacteria.

conveyor belt (kuhn-VAY-ur BELT): A conveyor belt is a moving belt that takes materials from one place to another in a factory. Ice cream containers move through the factory on a conveyor belt.

expires (ek-SPIREZ): Something expires when it reaches the end of the time it can be used. Ice cream expires after a certain date.

homogenized (huh-MOJ-uh-nized): Food is homogenized when the cream in it is broken into small bits and spread evenly in the liquid. Ice cream mix is homogenized at the factory.

ice crystals (ICE KRISS-tuhlz): Ice crystals are a solid form of water that can be sandy in ice cream. Stabilizers stop ice crystals from forming in ice cream.

ingredient (in-GREE-dee-uhnt): An ingredient is something that is added to a mixture, like one item in a recipe list. Milk is the main ingredient in ice cream.

pasteurized (PASS-chuh-rized): Food is pasteurized when it is heated to a high temperature and harmful bacteria is killed. Ice cream needs to be pasteurized.

skimmed (SKIMD): Skimmed milk is milk that has had the cream removed. Skimmed milk is used in ice cream mix.

stabilizers (STAY-buhl-ize-erz): Stabilizers are an ingredient that stop ice crystals from forming in ice cream. Stabilizers are added to the ice cream mix.

tanker truck (TANG-kur TRUHK): A tanker truck is a truck that is used to move liquids or gasses from one place to another. Milk goes to the ice cream factory in a tanker truck.

BOOKS

Older, Jules. *Ice Cream.* Watertown, MA: Charlesbridge, 2002.

Rosenberg, Pam. *How Did That Get to My Table? Ice Cream.* Ann Arbor, MI: Cherry Lake, 2010.

Snyder, Inez. *Milk to Ice Cream.* New York: Welcome Books/ Children's Press, 2003.

INDEX

Visit our Web site for links about ice cream production: childsworld.com/links

Note to Parents, Teachers, and Librarians: We routinely verify our Web links to make sure they are safe and active sites. So encourage your readers to check them out!